MW01148497

ALEX,

THE PRESENT IS A
GIFT!

THANK YOU FOR BEING
A GROUNDING FORCE
ON THE FARM :)

- SALLY

the POWER of PRESENCE

By Sally Celigoy

Did you know you have a
superpower?

It's with you everywhere you go.

It's called the

POWER OF PRESENCE

and you can practice by
taking life slow.

Oftentimes, you are living in
the future or the past.

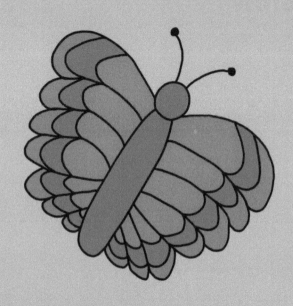

You might be thinking about the lunch you ate, or how you can't wait to get out of class.

when you use the
POWER of PRESENCE,
you live in the
present moment...

which is what you're experiencing
right here, right now!

**There are many ways to practice.
Let me show you how.**

Breathing is a simple way to use
your superpower.

Take a deep breath in and imagine
you're smelling a flower.

Now breathe out and pretend you're
blowing out candles on a cake.

Try this a few more times,
and pay attention to each
breath you take.

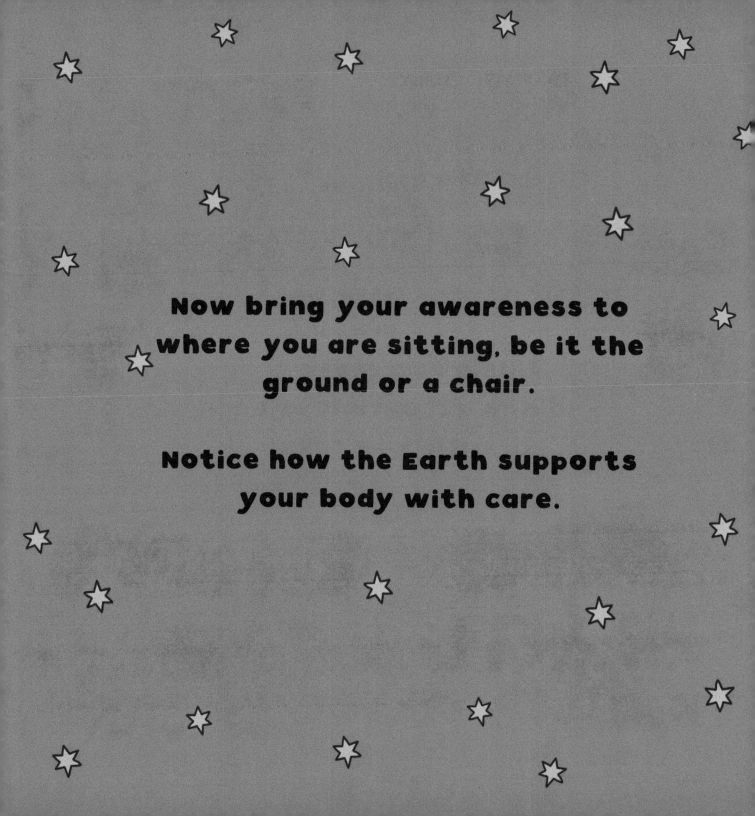

Now bring your awareness to where you are sitting, be it the ground or a chair.

Notice how the Earth supports your body with care.

Feel your legs grow heavy and let them sink into the ground.

You are present in this moment, safe and sound.

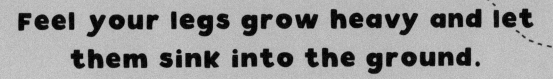

Now use your superpower to focus on what you hear.

You might hear rain falling,
dogs barking, people chatting
far or near.

Listen carefully, and you will discover more sounds.

Like the buzzing of bees, or the whistling of wind all around.

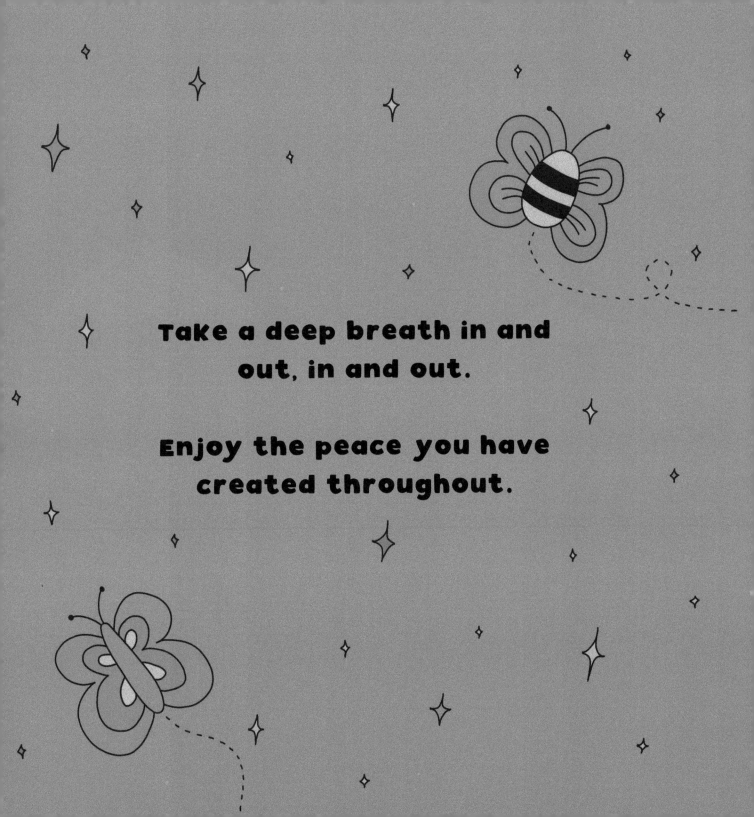

Take a deep breath in and
out, in and out.

Enjoy the peace you have
created throughout.

Take another deep breath
in and out, in and out.

This is what
the POWER of PRESENCE
is all about!

CPSIA information can be obtained
at www.ICGtesting.com
Printed in the USA
BVHW020346220521
607795BV00007B/1456